Authentic Indian Recip

Two from the Subcontinent

Simple and Satisfying Indian Dishes for Busy Couples

BY Yannick Alcorn

Copyright Warnings

Table of Contents

Introduction

"Authentic Indian Recipes for Two" brings you and your special someone the very best of Indian cuisine to savor together. In this cookbook, you'll find 30 remarkable recipes that capture the diverse flavors that make Indian food so delectable.

Celebrate special occasions and everyday meals with these aromatic feasts for two. With this cookbook, you can immerse your taste buds in India's culinary delights, from shareable appetizers to mains that showcase complex layers of spice to desserts that provide a perfect sweet finish. Each recipe promises a mouthwatering meal crafted for just the two of you.

So treat yourself and your loved one to the ultimate dining experience with the iconic flavors of India. These dishes are guaranteed to spice up date nights, anniversaries or any occasion that calls for extraordinary food shared with your favorite person.

1. Falooda

Yummy Indian ice cream dessert for two!

Duration: 20 Minutes

Prep Time: 15 Minutes

Serve: 2

List of Ingredients:

- 8 tbsp of cooked falooda sev
- 2 tbsp of syrup (rose)
- 2 tbsp of drained sweet basil seeds (soaked and rinsed)
- 2 handfuls of chopped pistachios
- 2 tbsp of sugar
- 450ml of chilled milk (full fat)
- 3 scoops of ice cream
- 3 tbsp of rose jelly

AAAAAAAAAAAAAAAAAAAAAAAA

Methods:

A. In a pan, boil the sugar and milk together until the sugar is completely dissolved.

B. Take 2 cups and add basil seeds to each cup. Then, add jelly and syrup to the cups.

C. Next, add the falooda sev to the cups.

D. Pour the previously prepared milk mixture over the ingredients in the cups.

E. Top it off with a scoop of ice cream and sprinkle chopped pistachios on top.

F. Finally, it's time to enjoy your zesty sour cocktail!

Cooking Notes:

A. Soaking the basil seeds: Before adding the basil seeds to the cups, soak them in water for about 10-15 minutes. The seeds will swell and become gelatinous, adding a unique texture to the cocktail. You can also soak them in flavored water, such as rose water or orange blossom water, for an extra layer of aroma.

B. Experiment with jelly flavors: The recipe mentions jelly, but you can explore various flavors like rose, mango, or strawberry jelly. Each flavor will bring its own delightful twist to the cocktail.

C. Syrup options: Consider using different syrups like rose syrup, khus (vetiver) syrup, or any other fruit-flavored syrup. These syrups will infuse the cocktail with their distinctive tastes and colors.

D. Falooda sev variations: While the recipe suggests using traditional falooda sev, you can also try using different types of noodles or vermicelli. Vermicelli made from rice, wheat, or even sweet potato can add diversity to the texture.

E. Infuse the milk: Before boiling the milk with sugar, you can infuse it with flavors like cardamom pods, saffron strands, or a cinnamon stick. Simmer the milk with these ingredients for a few minutes, then strain them out before adding the sugar.

F. Serving the cocktail cold: For a refreshing experience, chill the cocktail in the refrigerator for an hour or two before serving. This will make it more enjoyable, especially on a hot day.

G. Add a touch of rose water: To enhance the traditional falooda flavor, sprinkle a few drops of rose water on top of the cocktail just before serving. Rose water complements the ingredients and adds a lovely floral aroma.

H. Crushed ice option: If you prefer a colder and icier cocktail, serve it with crushed ice or ice cubes. The ice will keep the drink cold and maintain a delightful chill throughout.

I. Boozy twist: For an adult version of the cocktail, you can add a splash of rose or strawberry liqueur. However, please drink responsibly and ensure the cocktail is served to adults only.

J. Savoring the layers: When serving the cocktail, encourage your guests to mix the layers and flavors together for a harmonious taste. The blend of textures and tastes will make every sip enjoyable.

K. By incorporating these additional cooking notes, you can explore different flavors, textures, and presentations of the Basil Seed and Falooda Cocktail. Get creative and have fun experimenting with various combinations to craft a personalized and delightful drink!

2. Mint Lassi

Just so you know, you can have Lassi in mint flavor too!!

Duration: 03 Minutes

Prep Time: Nil

Serve: 2

List of Ingredients:

- 2 cups of yogurt
- 1 cup of mint leaves
- 2 tbsp of honey
- 1 cup of milk

AAAAAAAAAAAAAAAAAAAAAAA

Methods:

A. In a food processor, combine 2 cups of yogurt, 1 cup of mint leaves, 2 tbsp of honey, and 1 cup of milk.
B. Process all the ingredients until they are well blended and smooth.
C. Serve the Mint Lassi in glasses filled with ice for a refreshing and cooling treat.

Cooking Notes:

A. Adjust the sweetness of the Mint Lassi by adding more or less honey, depending on your taste preference.
B. For a thicker consistency, you can use Greek yogurt or strain regular yogurt using a cheesecloth before blending.
C. If you prefer a thinner Lassi, you can add more milk to achieve the desired consistency.
D. Garnish the Mint Lassi with a sprig of fresh mint leaves for an attractive presentation.
E. Feel free to add a pinch of ground cardamom or a dash of rose water for an extra layer of flavor.

3. Indian Summer Cocktail

For your Indian Summer Salad, you have the Indian Summer cocktail to enjoy with it!

Duration: 10 Minutes

Prep Time: Nil

Serve: 2

List of Ingredients:

- 1 ginger
- 100g of chopped mangoes
- 2 lime wedges for garnish
- 1 handful of ice cubes
- 20 ml of lemon juice
- 120 ml of vodka
- 50 ml of sweet and sour syrup
- 10 mint leaves

AAAAAAAAAAAAAAAAAAAAAAAA

Methods:

A. In a food processor, combine ginger, chopped mangoes, ice cubes, lemon juice, vodka, sweet and sour syrup, and mint leaves.

B. Blend all the ingredients together until smooth and well combined.

C. Serve the Indian Summer Cocktail in glasses and garnish each glass with lime wedges.

Cooking Notes:

A. You can adjust the sweetness and tartness of the cocktail by adding more or less sweet and sour syrup and lemon juice, according to your taste preference.

B. For a non-alcoholic version, you can omit the vodka and replace it with sparkling water or lemon-lime soda.

C. If you prefer a more intense ginger flavor, you can increase the amount of ginger used in the recipe or add a pinch of ground ginger.

D. To make the cocktail even more refreshing, you can muddle the mint leaves with a splash of lemon juice before adding them to the food processor. This will release more of the mint's aroma and flavor.

E. For an extra tropical twist, you can add a splash of pineapple juice or coconut milk to the cocktail.

4. Watermelon Juice

This is one fruit juice that people hardly crave, but not when you have this tantalizing Indian version.

Duration: 05 Minutes

Prep Time: Nil

Serve: 2

List of Ingredients:

- 1 tbsp of sabja seeds (soaked, rinsed, drained)
- 2 tbsp of lemon juice
- 6 cups of deseeded chopped watermelon

AAAAAAAAAAAAAAAAAAAAAAA

Methods:

A. Start by blending fresh watermelon pieces along with some lemon juice until you get a smooth and well-mixed juice.
B. Prepare glasses filled with ice cubes, and pour the freshly blended watermelon juice into the glasses.
C. Finally, garnish each glass of watermelon juice with sabja seeds for added texture and visual appeal.

Cooking Notes:

A. For the best watermelon juice, use ripe and juicy watermelon. You can also chill the watermelon in the refrigerator before blending to make the juice more refreshing.

B. Watermelon presentation: To elevate the visual appeal of the watermelon juice, consider serving it in hollowed-out watermelon shells. Scoop out the flesh of a watermelon, leaving a thin layer intact, and pour the freshly blended juice back into the shell. This creative presentation will impress your guests and make it a centerpiece on the table.

C. Freezing the watermelon: For an icy and slushy texture, freeze the watermelon pieces before blending. Spread the watermelon cubes in a single layer on a baking sheet and freeze them for a few hours or until solid. The frozen watermelon will result in a frostier and more refreshing juice.

D. Infusing with herbs: Besides mint, you can experiment with other herbs to infuse the watermelon juice with unique flavors. Try adding a sprig of basil, a few lavender buds, or a pinch of rosemary while blending. These herbal infusions can take the juice to a whole new level.

E. Fruity variations: While watermelon alone makes a refreshing juice, you can mix it with other fruits for exciting flavor combinations. Try blending watermelon with strawberries, raspberries, or even a splash of orange juice for a fruity medley.

F. Coconut water addition: For a hydrating twist, replace some of the water in the blender with coconut water. This will not only add subtle coconut flavor but also provide additional electrolytes and hydration.

G. A touch of ginger: Add a small piece of fresh ginger to the blender for a hint of spiciness and zing. Ginger pairs exceptionally well with watermelon and adds a lively kick to the juice.

H. Watermelon popsicles: If you have leftover watermelon juice, pour it into popsicle molds and freeze them. These watermelon popsicles will be a refreshing treat on hot summer days.

I. Sparkling watermelon spritzer: Mix the freshly blended watermelon juice with sparkling water to create a sparkling watermelon spritzer. The bubbles will add effervescence and make the juice even more delightful.

J. Agave or honey sweetener: If you prefer alternative sweeteners, you can use agave syrup or honey instead of sugar. These natural sweeteners will complement the watermelon's flavor without overpowering it.

K. Watermelon mocktail: Turn the watermelon juice into a mocktail by adding a splash of cranberry juice or grenadine for a vibrant color and a hint of tartness.

L. By incorporating these additional cooking notes, you can customize the Watermelon Juice recipe to suit your preferences and create refreshing variations that you and your guests will thoroughly enjoy. Whether it's a simple and classic watermelon juice or an elaborately infused concoction, savor the fresh taste of this summer delight!

5. Nimbu Pani

Refreshing lemonade recipe. Just for you!

Duration: 04 Minutes

Prep Time: Nil

Serve: 2

List of Ingredients:

- 1 pinch of black salt
- 2 tbsp of sugar
- 1 handful of mint leaves
- 2 cups of ice cubes
- 2 cups of lemon juice

AAAAAAAAAAAAAAAAAAAAAAA

Methods:

A. In a large jar, combine the lemon juice, sugar, and a pinch of black salt. Mix well until the sugar and salt dissolve.
B. Prepare glasses filled with ice cubes.
C. Pour the Nimbu Pani into the glasses over the ice cubes. Garnish each glass with a few fresh mint leaves for added freshness and aroma.
D. Now, it's time to enjoy the refreshing and tangy Nimbu Pani!

Cooking Notes:

A. For the best taste, use freshly squeezed lemon juice. Bottled lemon juice may have added preservatives and lack the same fresh flavor.

B. Adjust the sweetness of the Nimbu Pani according to your taste preference by adding more or less sugar.

C. Black salt, also known as kala namak, is a type of rock salt that adds a unique and slightly sulfuric taste to the drink. If you can't find black salt, you can substitute it with regular table salt, but the flavor will be slightly different.

D. Feel free to customize the drink by adding a pinch of ground cumin (jeera) or a splash of roasted cumin powder. This will give the Nimbu Pani an extra depth of flavor.

E. You can also add a dash of chaat masala for a tangy and spicy twist to the drink.

F. To make a sparkling version of Nimbu Pani, you can add a splash of club soda or sparkling water to the mixture.

G. If you like a bit of heat, you can finely chop some green chilies and add them to the Nimbu Pani for a spicy kick.

H. Nimbu Pani is a versatile drink, and you can experiment with other herbs like basil or coriander leaves to add different herbal notes to the beverage.

6. Papaya Lassi

Who would have thought that Lassi can be enjoyed in papaya flavor too?

Duration: 03 Minutes

Prep Time: Nil

Serve: 2

List of Ingredients:

- 1 cup of chopped papaya
- 1 pinch of cardamom
- 1 tbsp of honey
- 1 cup of milk
- 1 cup of yogurt

AAAAAAAAAAAAAAAAAAAAAAA

Methods:

A. In a blender, combine chopped papaya, cardamom, honey, milk, and yogurt.

B. Blend all the ingredients together until you get a smooth and creamy consistency.

C. Serve the Papaya Lassi in glasses filled with ice for a refreshing and cooling drink.

Cooking Notes:

A. Use ripe and sweet papaya for the best flavor and natural sweetness in the Lassi.

B. If you don't have cardamom, you can use a pinch of ground cinnamon as a substitute. It will add a warm and aromatic flavor to the drink.

C. Adjust the sweetness of the Papaya Lassi by adding more or less honey according to your taste preference.

D. For a thicker and creamier Lassi, you can use Greek yogurt or strain regular yogurt using a cheesecloth before blending.

E. If you prefer a thinner consistency, you can add more milk to achieve the desired thickness.

F. Feel free to garnish the Papaya Lassi with a sprinkle of ground cardamom or a few slices of fresh papaya for an attractive presentation.

G. To make it more tropical, you can add a splash of coconut milk or coconut water to the blender along with the other ingredients.

H. Papaya Lassi is a versatile drink, and you can experiment with other spices like ginger or nutmeg to add different flavor dimensions to the beverage.

I. Serve the Papaya Lassi immediately after blending to enjoy its fresh and fruity taste. You can also refrigerate any leftovers and consume them within a day for the best flavor and nutritional benefits.

7. Indian Lassi

Sip on this sweet Indian mango drink and enjoy quality time with your special one.

Duration: 05 Minutes

Prep Time: Nil

Serve: 2

List of Ingredients:

- 1 tsp of salt
- 2 handfuls of ice cubes
- 1 pinch of cardamom
- 2 cups of Greek yogurt

AAAAAAAAAAAAAAAAAAAAAAAA

Methods:

A. In a blender, combine the Greek yogurt, salt, a pinch of cardamom, and ice cubes.
B. Blend all the ingredients together until you get a smooth and creamy consistency.
C. Serve the Indian Lassi immediately in glasses, and enjoy its refreshing and cooling taste.

Cooking Notes:

A. Greek yogurt is thicker and creamier compared to regular yogurt, making it ideal for a rich and luxurious Lassi. However, you can use regular yogurt if Greek yogurt is not available.

B. Adjust the amount of salt according to your taste preference. Some people prefer a slightly salty Lassi, while others prefer it sweeter. Start with a small amount and add more if desired.

C. Cardamom adds a delightful and aromatic flavor to the Lassi. You can use ground cardamom or crush whole cardamom pods to get the pinch of cardamom needed for the recipe.

D. For a sweeter version, you can add a tablespoon or more of honey, sugar, or any other sweetener of your choice. Adjust the sweetness to suit your taste.

E. For a tropical twist, you can add a splash of rose water or a few drops of kewra essence. This will give the Lassi a lovely floral aroma and taste.

F. If you prefer a fruity Lassi, you can add some ripe mango, strawberries, or other fruits to the blender along with the other ingredients. This will result in a delicious and fruity Mango Lassi or Strawberry Lassi.

G. For a vegan version, you can use dairy-free yogurt made from almond, coconut, or soy milk. Make sure to choose a yogurt with a similar thickness to Greek yogurt to achieve the desired creamy texture.

H. Lassi is best served immediately after blending while it's still frothy and cold. You can also chill the Lassi in the refrigerator before serving if you prefer it extra cold.

8. Cauliflower Green Curry

Need Indian comfort food for two? This meal is here to serve you some Green Curry awesomeness!

Duration: 20 Minutes

Prep Time: 25 Minutes

Serve: 2

List of Ingredients:

- 1 tbsp of coconut oil
- 3 tbsp of green curry paste
- 1 tsp of coconut sugar
- 1 tbsp of lemon juice
- 2 cups of chopped spinach
- 1 tbsp of chopped ginger
- 3 tbsp of moong dal (soaked and drained)
- 1 sliced shallots
- 1 minced garlic clove
- 1 cup of chopped cauliflower
- 1 tbsp of tamari
- 7 oz of coconut milk

For serving

- 2 lemon wedges
- 2 handfuls of roasted cashews
- 1 handful of chopped cilantro

AAAAAAAAAAAAAAAAAAAAAAAA

Methods:

A. Heat coconut oil in a pan and sauté minced garlic, chopped ginger, and sliced shallots until fragrant.

B. Add the green curry paste to the pan and cook for about a minute to release its flavors.

C. Toss in the chopped cauliflower and cook for an additional 2 minutes before pouring in the coconut milk. Let it simmer for a few minutes before adding the soaked and drained moong dal, tamari, and coconut sugar.

D. Continue cooking the curry for approximately 10 more minutes until the cauliflower and moong dal are tender and well-cooked.

E. Serve the cauliflower green curry with rice and garnish it with lemon wedges, roasted cashews, and chopped cilantro.

Cooking notes:

A. Coconut oil is ideal for making green curry as it enhances the coconut flavor and complements the other ingredients.

B. While sautéing the garlic, ginger, and shallot, ensure not to burn them; cook until they become aromatic and lightly browned.

C. Green curry paste is the primary flavoring agent. Adjust the quantity based on your preferred spice level and the intensity of the paste.

D. Before adding the cauliflower, make sure it's chopped into bite-sized pieces to ensure even cooking and easier eating.

E. Simmering the coconut milk allows it to infuse with the other flavors in the curry, creating a creamy and delicious base.

F. Soaking the moong dal beforehand helps it cook faster and more evenly.

G. Tamari is a gluten-free alternative to soy sauce, providing a savory umami taste to the curry. Adjust the quantity to suit your taste.

H. Coconut sugar adds a subtle sweetness that balances the spicy and savory elements of the green curry.

I. During the 10-minute cooking time, stir the curry occasionally to prevent sticking and ensure even distribution of flavors.

J. The garnishes - lemon wedges, roasted cashews, and chopped cilantro - add freshness, tanginess, and crunch to the dish, enhancing its overall appeal.

K. This cauliflower green curry pairs well with jasmine rice or brown rice, but you can choose any type of rice you prefer. Enjoy the flavorful and comforting meal!

9. Chicken Madras Curry

Forget ordering this meal from a restaurant, the homemade version tastes much better.

Duration: 10 Minutes

Prep Time: 20 Minutes

Serve: 2

List of Ingredients:

- 1 tsp of ground coriander
- 1 tsp of ground cumin
- 1 tsp of vegetable oil
- 1 pinch of turmeric
- 1 quartered onion
- 1 tbsp of chili powder
- 1 handful of chopped coriander
- 200g of chopped tomatoes
- 1 minced garlic clove
- 1 chopped red chili
- 1 peeled ginger
- 2 chunked chicken breasts

AAAAAAAAAAAAAAAAAAAAAAAA

Methods:

A. Use a blender to process garlic, ginger, onion, and red chili into a coarse paste.

B. Heat vegetable oil in a pan and add the paste. Stir-fry the paste until it's cooked.

C. Add the ground coriander, ground cumin, turmeric, and chili powder to the pan. Mix well with the paste.

D. Put the quartered onion and chopped tomatoes into the pan along with the chunked chicken breasts. Cook everything together until the chicken is fully cooked and all the ingredients are well incorporated.

E. Garnish the Chicken Madras Curry with chopped coriander and serve it with rice.

Cooking notes:

A. When processing the garlic, ginger, onion, and red chili in the blender, avoid over-blending, as a coarse paste will provide more texture to the curry.

B. Use a pan or skillet with enough surface area to comfortably cook all the ingredients together.

C. When stir-frying the paste in the pan, make sure to do it over medium heat to prevent burning and ensure even cooking.

D. Adjust the amount of chili powder based on your spice preference. You can increase or decrease the quantity to make the curry milder or hotter.

E. Cooking the chicken until it's fully done is essential for safety and taste. Ensure there are no pink parts in the chicken before serving.

F. You can customize the level of spiciness by adding or reducing the amount of red chili used in the paste.

G. For a creamier texture, you can add a splash of coconut milk to the curry during cooking.

H. The chopped coriander adds a fresh and aromatic touch to the dish, enhancing its overall flavor profile.

I. Serve the Chicken Madras Curry with steamed white rice or fragrant basmati rice for a delicious and satisfying meal. You can also pair it with naan or roti for a traditional Indian dining experience. Enjoy the rich and flavorful curry!

10. Coconut Butter Cauliflower

This delicious food will make you fall in love with it!

Duration: 10 Minutes

Prep Time: 10 Minutes

Serve: 2

List of Ingredients:

- 1 tbsp of salt
- 2 minced garlic cloves
- 1 pinch of turmeric
- 1 tsp of garam masala
- 1 handful of chopped yellow onion
- 1 handful of chopped cilantro
- 1 tbsp of coconut oil
- 1 tbsp of pepper
- 1 cup of coconut milk
- 1 tbsp of olive oil
- 1 tsp of curry powder
- 1 chopped cauliflower head
- 1 grated ginger
- 3 ounces of tomato paste
- 1 pinch of cayenne pepper

AAAAAAAAAAAAAAAAAAAAAAA

Methods:

A. Preheat the oven to 422 degrees F (214 degrees C).

B. Spray a baking sheet with cooking spray to prevent sticking.

C. In a bowl, combine part of the minced garlic, part of the minced ginger, part of the coconut milk, cauliflower, and salt. Allow the cauliflower to marinate in this mixture.

D. Layer the marinated cauliflower mixture on the prepared baking sheet.

E. Bake the cauliflower in the preheated oven for about 4 minutes until it's partially cooked.

F. In a pan, sauté chopped onion in oil until it becomes translucent and slightly browned.

G. Add the remaining minced ginger and garlic to the sautéed onion and cook for an additional 4 minutes.

H. Mix in the cayenne pepper, garam masala, turmeric, and curry powder, stirring well to combine the spices with the onion mixture.

I. Pour in the remaining coconut milk and coconut paste to create a thick sauce. Let it simmer until the sauce reaches the desired consistency.

J. Stir in the coconut oil and the partially baked cauliflower mixture into the sauce, ensuring they are well coated.

K. Add sliced bell pepper, chopped cilantro, and additional salt if needed for seasoning.

L. Serve the Coconut Butter Cauliflower and enjoy this flavorful and creamy dish.

Cooking notes:

A. Preheating the oven to the specified temperature ensures that the cauliflower cooks evenly and becomes tender while retaining its texture.

B. Marinating the cauliflower with garlic, ginger, coconut milk, and salt imparts flavors to the vegetable, enhancing its taste.

C. Baking the cauliflower for a short time before adding it to the sauce ensures that it's partially cooked and will finish cooking in the sauce, absorbing the flavors of the dish.

D. Sautéing the onion in the pan with oil helps to release its sweetness and build the base flavor for the curry sauce.

E. When adding the spices (cayenne, garam masala, turmeric, curry powder), make sure to stir them well with the onion and garlic mixture to evenly distribute the flavors.

F. The coconut milk and coconut paste create a rich and creamy sauce that coats the cauliflower and infuses it with delicious coconut flavor.

G. Adjust the amount of cayenne pepper based on your preferred level of spiciness.

H. The addition of coconut oil provides additional richness and a smooth texture to the sauce.

I. The bell pepper and cilantro add freshness and color to the dish, enhancing its visual appeal.

J. You can serve this Coconut Butter Cauliflower as a main course with steamed rice or as a side dish to complement other Indian-inspired dishes. Enjoy the delightful taste of this creamy and aromatic cauliflower curry!

11. Chickpea Curry

Are you and your special one on a vegan diet? Then this Indian curry chickpea meal suits your diet just fine!!

Duration: 05 Minutes

Prep Time: 15 Minutes

Serve: 2

List of Ingredients:

- 1 tsp of minced garlic
- 1 pinch of cayenne pepper
- 1 pinch of turmeric
- 1 pinch of ground coriander
- 200g of drained chickpeas
- 200ml of coconut milk
- 200 ml of chopped tomatoes
- 1 pinch of cumin
- 1 tsp of garam masala
- 1 small-sized chopped onion
- 1 tbsp of oil
- 1 tbsp of salt
- 1 tbsp of pepper
- 1 tsp of coconut sugar

AAAAAAAAAAAAAAAAAAAAAAA

Methods:

A. In a pan with oil, sauté cayenne pepper, garam masala, garlic, cumin, onion, turmeric, and coriander.
B. Cook the spices and onions for 3 minutes to develop their flavors.
C. Add coconut milk, chickpeas, and tomatoes to the pan.
D. Cook the mixture for 7 minutes, allowing the flavors to blend.
E. Season the curry with pepper, salt, and sugar for a balanced taste.
F. Serve the Chickpea Curry with rice.
G. Enjoy this flavorful and hearty dish!

Cooking notes:

A. Use a wide pan or skillet to accommodate all the ingredients comfortably.

B. Sautéing the spices and aromatics in oil helps to release their flavors and aromas, enhancing the overall taste of the curry.

C. Adjust the amount of cayenne pepper based on your preferred level of spiciness. You can increase or decrease it to suit your taste.

D. While sautéing the onions and spices, stir them frequently to prevent burning and ensure even cooking.

E. Coconut milk adds creaminess and richness to the curry. You can use canned or fresh coconut milk based on availability and preference.

F. Chickpeas are the main ingredient in this curry and should be cooked until they are tender. If using canned chickpeas, make sure to drain and rinse them before adding to the curry.

G. The tomatoes provide acidity and balance to the dish. You can use fresh tomatoes or canned diced tomatoes depending on your preference.

H. Season the curry with salt, pepper, and sugar to enhance the flavors and create a harmonious taste profile. Taste and adjust the seasoning according to your liking.

I. Serve the Chickpea Curry with steamed white rice, basmati rice, or naan bread for a complete and satisfying meal.

J. Garnish the dish with chopped fresh cilantro or parsley for added freshness and color.

K. This Chickpea Curry is a delicious and nutritious vegetarian option that can be enjoyed as a main course or as a side dish. It's packed with protein, fiber, and a medley of spices that create a delightful Indian-inspired flavor.

12. Indian Rose

Cool off the heat of summer with glasses of this delicious rose drink!!

Duration: 07 Minutes

Prep Time: Nil

Serve: 2

List of Ingredients:

- 1 tbsp of sugar
- 1 handful of rose petals for garnish
- 1 tsp of rose water
- 2 cups of milk
- 1 tbsp of soaked and rinsed sabja seeds (drained)
- 4 tbsp of rose syrup

AAAAAAAAAAAAAAAAAAAAAAAA

Methods:

A. In a bowl, combine sugar and milk, and mix them well until the sugar dissolves.

B. Add the syrup to the mixture, followed by the rose water for a fragrant and floral flavor.

C. Finish the Indian Rose by adding the seeds, which add texture and extra taste.

D. Serve the drink and garnish it with rose petals for an elegant presentation.

Cooking notes:

A. The sugar should be fully dissolved in the milk to avoid graininess in the final drink.

B. When adding the rose water, start with a small amount and taste the mixture before adding more. Rose water can be quite potent, and a little goes a long way.

C. The syrup can be store-bought or homemade. Rose syrup or Rooh Afza is commonly used in Indian rose-flavored drinks and desserts.

D. For the seeds, you can use chia seeds or basil seeds (Sabja seeds). These seeds add a unique texture to the drink, similar to small tapioca pearls.

E. Garnishing with rose petals adds a touch of elegance and reinforces the rose flavor of the drink.

F. Indian Rose is best served chilled, so you can refrigerate it for a while before serving or add ice cubes to the drink.

G. Feel free to adjust the sweetness and rose flavor to your preference. You can also experiment with adding a splash of fresh lemon juice for a hint of tanginess.

H. This refreshing and delightful Indian Rose drink is perfect for quenching your thirst on a hot day or enjoying as a special treat with its exotic rose-infused taste. Enjoy this beautiful and aromatic beverage!

13. Banana Lassi

You and your special one can enjoy Lassi in Banana flavor too!

Duration: 07 Minutes

Prep Time: Nil

Serve: 2

List of Ingredients:

- 2 handfuls of ice cubes
- 2 cups of chopped ripe bananas
- 2 cups of Greek yogurt
- 1 cup of milk
- 1 tbsp of sugar

AAAAAAAAAAAAAAAAAAAAAAA

Methods:

A. In a food processor, combine the ice cubes, chopped ripe bananas, Greek yogurt, milk, and sugar.
B. Process the ingredients well until you achieve a smooth and creamy consistency.
C. Serve the Banana Lassi and enjoy this delicious and refreshing beverage.

Cooking notes:

A. Use ripe and sweet bananas for the best flavor in the Banana Lassi.

B. Greek yogurt adds creaminess and tanginess to the lassi. You can use plain yogurt as an alternative, but Greek yogurt provides a thicker and richer texture.

C. Adjust the amount of sugar based on your taste preference and the sweetness of the bananas. You can also use honey or maple syrup as a natural sweetener.

D. You can add a pinch of ground cardamom or a splash of rose water for an exotic twist to the Banana Lassi.

E. If you prefer a thinner consistency, you can add more milk to the lassi. Conversely, if you want it thicker, reduce the amount of milk or use less ice cubes.

F. The ice cubes help in achieving a chilled and refreshing lassi. However, you can skip them if you prefer a less cold beverage.

G. Garnish the Banana Lassi with a sprinkle of ground cinnamon or a few slices of banana for an attractive presentation.

H. This Banana Lassi is a delightful and healthy drink that can be enjoyed as a breakfast smoothie, a midday snack, or a cooling treat on a hot day. It's packed with vitamins, probiotics, and natural sweetness from the bananas. Savor the creamy and fruity goodness of this easy-to-make lassi!

14. Mango Chicken Curry

Chicken prepared in mango curry tastes heavenly!

Duration: 15 Minutes

Prep Time: 25 Minutes

Serve: 2

List of Ingredients:

- 1 tsp of fennel seeds
- 1 minced clove garlic
- 1 sliced onion
- 1 tsp of chili powder
- 3 tbsp of yogurt
- 1 tsp of red chili

For the curry

- 1 tbsp of oil
- 1 tsp of garam masala
- 1 tsp of ground coriander
- 3 tbsp of tomato puree
- chopped garlic
- 4 tbsp of coconut cream
- 1 diced mango
- 1 cinnamon stick
- 200g of diced chicken thigh
- 3 cardamom pods
- 1 tbsp of salt
- 1 diced onion

AAAAAAAAAAAAAAAAAAAAAAAA

Methods:

A. In a blender, combine fennel seeds, minced garlic, sliced onion, chili powder, yogurt, and red chili to make a paste. Blend well until smooth.

B. Take half of the paste and marinate the diced chicken thigh. Set it aside for later use.

C. In a pan with oil, sauté cardamom pods and cinnamon stick for about 2 minutes to release their flavors.

D. Add the curry paste to the pan and cook for 4 minutes to allow the spices to develop their aromas.

E. Stir in the diced onion, ground coriander, garam masala, and chopped garlic. Then, add the tomato puree to enrich the curry's base.

F. Pour in the coconut cream and cook for 4 minutes, stirring the mixture to create a creamy and flavorful sauce.

G. Add the diced mango, remaining paste, and marinated chicken to the pan. Allow the curry to simmer for approximately 15 minutes, ensuring the chicken is fully cooked and infused with the curry's flavors.

H. Serve the Mango Chicken Curry with steamed rice for a delicious and satisfying meal.

Cooking notes:

A. Fennel seeds offer a unique flavor and fragrance to the curry. If unavailable, you can substitute with ground fennel for a similar taste.

B. Marinating the chicken in the paste enhances its taste and tenderizes the meat during the cooking process.

C. Sautéing the cardamom and cinnamon in oil helps to release their essential oils and adds aromatic undertones to the curry.

D. When cooking the curry paste, stir frequently to prevent burning and ensure even distribution of flavors.

E. Garam masala and ground coriander contribute warm and earthy notes to the curry, while the tomato puree adds acidity and a rich base.

F. Coconut cream adds creaminess and a subtle sweetness to the curry, balancing the spices and enhancing the mango flavor.

G. Adjust the level of spiciness by modifying the amount of chili powder and red chili to suit your preference.

H. Simmering the curry for 15 minutes allows the flavors to meld and ensures the chicken is thoroughly cooked and tender.

I. Mango provides a natural sweetness and tropical twist to the curry. Use ripe and sweet mangoes for the best taste.

J. This Mango Chicken Curry is a delightful fusion of spices and fruity flavors, making it a fantastic choice for those who enjoy a combination of savory and sweet notes in their dishes. Enjoy this aromatic and flavorful curry with a side of rice for a satisfying meal!

15. Maharashtrian Taak

You should try this!!

Duration: 04 Minutes

Prep Time: Nil

Serve: 2

List of Ingredients:

- 1 tsp of salt
- 200 ml of water
- 1 handful of chopped coriander
- 1 tbsp of cumin powder
- 1 tsp of chopped green chili
- 1 chopped ginger
- 150 ml of yogurt

AAAAAAAAAAAAAAAAAAAAAAA

Methods:

A. In a blender, combine yogurt, chili, water, ginger, and salt.
B. Blend the ingredients well until you get a smooth mixture, and then strain it into a jug to remove any coarse bits.
C. Add ground coriander and cumin to the strained mixture and mix well to incorporate the flavors.
D. Serve the Maharashtrian Taak and enjoy this refreshing and spiced buttermilk drink.

Cooking notes:

A. Maharashtrian Taak is a traditional buttermilk drink from the Indian state of Maharashtra, known for its tangy and spiced flavor profile.

B. Use plain yogurt for the base of the Taak. You can adjust the level of spiciness by adding more or fewer chilies based on your taste preference.

C. Ginger adds a zesty kick to the Taak. You can grate the ginger before blending it with the other ingredients.

D. Straining the mixture after blending ensures a smooth and consistent texture for the drink, free from any fibrous bits.

E. Ground coriander and cumin add a depth of flavor to the Taak and enhance its overall taste. You can toast the coriander and cumin seeds before grinding them for an extra layer of aroma.

F. Adjust the salt to your liking, but be mindful not to oversalt the Taak.

G. Maharashtrian Taak is often served as a cooling and refreshing beverage during hot weather or as an accompaniment to spicy dishes. It aids in digestion and provides a cooling effect to the palate.

H. You can serve the Taak chilled by refrigerating it before serving or add ice cubes to the drink.

I. Garnish the Taak with a sprig of fresh coriander or mint leaves for a touch of green and an appealing presentation.

J. Enjoy the Maharashtrian Taak as a thirst-quenching and flavorful drink with your meals or as a light and healthy beverage on its own.

16. Butter Chicken Curry

Curried chicken is an amazing meal all by itself, now, adding butter to the mix just takes this meal to a whole new level!!

Duration: 15 Minutes

Prep Time: 25 Minutes

Serve: 2

List of Ingredients:

- 1 chopped cauliflower
- 1 crushed garlic clove
- 1 chopped shallot
- 1 pinch of cumin
- 1 pinch of turmeric
- 1 pinch of coriander
- 2 boneless chopped chicken breasts (skinless)
- 1 tbsp of lemon juice
- 100g of baby spinach leaves
- 4 tbsp of Greek yogurt
- 1 pinch of salt
- 1 sliced carrot (peeled)
- 1 tbsp of oil
- 1 tbsp of butter curry spice blend
- 1 tbsp of grated ginger
- 1 cup of chopped tomatoes (peeled)
- 70g of green beans
- 1 handful of chopped cilantro

AAAAAAAAAAAAAAAAAAAAAAA

Methods:

A. Preheat the oven to 372 degrees F (190 degrees C).

B. Layer a baking sheet with carrot and cauliflower on the bottom.

C. Drizzle a dash of oil, sprinkle pepper, and salt over the vegetables.

D. Roast the vegetables in the oven for approximately 20 minutes until tender and slightly browned.

E. In a pan with oil, sauté the onion for about 2 minutes until it becomes translucent.

F. Add the spices, ginger, and garlic to the pan and cook for 1 minute to release their aromas.

G. Stir in the tomatoes and cook for 5 minutes until they soften and form a sauce-like consistency.

H. Add the chicken pieces and beans to the pan, followed by the roasted carrot and cauliflower mixture. Mix everything well to coat the chicken and vegetables with the flavorful sauce.

I. Pour in the yogurt, add spinach, and squeeze lemon juice into the pan. Stir the mixture and continue cooking for another 3 minutes until the chicken is fully cooked and the spinach wilts.

J. Serve the Butter Chicken Curry with your choice of rice, naan bread, or roti for a complete and satisfying meal.

Cooking notes:

A. Preheating the oven ensures even cooking of the vegetables and enhances their flavors.

B. Cutting the carrot and cauliflower into similar-sized pieces allows them to cook evenly during roasting.

C. When roasting the vegetables, keep an eye on them to avoid overcooking or burning. Stirring the vegetables halfway through the roasting time ensures even browning.

D. Use a mix of aromatic spices such as garam masala, turmeric, cumin, and coriander to create a rich and flavorful curry base.

E. Incorporating yogurt in the curry adds a creamy texture and a tangy taste to balance the spices.

F. You can use boneless chicken thighs or breasts for the dish. Cut the chicken into bite-sized pieces to ensure quick and even cooking.

G. Add additional vegetables like bell peppers, peas, or potatoes for more variety and nutrition.

H. Adjust the level of spiciness by increasing or decreasing the amount of chili powder or adding fresh chili peppers according to your taste preference.

I. Garnish the Butter Chicken Curry with chopped cilantro or a dollop of yogurt for an attractive presentation and added freshness.

J. This popular Butter Chicken Curry recipe is a delightful combination of tender chicken, roasted vegetables, and aromatic spices, creating a mouthwatering and comforting dish. Enjoy the flavors of India with this hearty and delicious curry!

17. Indian Raita

It's refreshingly Indian!!

Duration: 02 Minutes

Prep Time: Nil

Serve: 2

List of Ingredients:

- 1 cup of chopped cucumber
- 1 tbsp of ground coriander
- 2 handfuls of chopped cilantro
- 1 tbsp of ground cumin
- 1 cup of yogurt
- 1 tbsp of chopped green onions

AAAAAAAAAAAAAAAAAAAAAAAA

Methods:

A. In a big bowl, combine the chopped cucumber, ground coriander, chopped cilantro, ground cumin, yogurt, and chopped green onions.
B. Stir all the ingredients well until they are thoroughly mixed.
C. Serve the Indian Raita and enjoy this refreshing and flavorful yogurt-based side dish.

Cooking notes:

A. Indian Raita is a popular accompaniment in Indian cuisine, served alongside spicy dishes to cool down the palate.

B. Use fresh and crisp cucumbers for the best texture in the Raita. You can peel and deseed a cucumber if desired, but it's not necessary.

C. Ground coriander and cumin add a fragrant and aromatic taste to the Raita. Toasting the whole seeds before grinding them can enhance their flavors further.

D. The cilantro adds a fresh and herbal note to the Raita. Make sure to wash the cilantro thoroughly and chop it finely.

E. Greek yogurt or plain yogurt works well for this recipe. Greek yogurt is thicker and creamier, while plain yogurt has a lighter consistency. You can use either based on your preference.

F. Adjust the amount of ground coriander and cumin to suit your taste. You can also add a pinch of red chili powder or black pepper for a hint of spiciness, if desired.

G. Green onions add a mild onion flavor to the Raita. You can use both the green and white parts of the onions.

H. You can refrigerate the Raita for a while before serving to let the flavors meld together and make it more refreshing.

I. Indian Raita pairs well with a variety of dishes, such as biryani, kebabs, and curry. It helps to balance the heat of spicy dishes and adds a cooling element to the meal.

J. Garnish the Raita with a sprinkle of ground coriander or cumin and a few cilantro leaves for an appealing presentation.

K. Enjoy the Indian Raita as a delightful and soothing side dish that complements the flavors of Indian cuisine. It's a simple and quick recipe to add a refreshing touch to your meals!

18. Indian Winter Soup

The Perfect Indian soup for winter!

Duration: 04 Minutes

Prep Time: 15 Minutes

Serve: 2

List of Ingredients:

- 1 cup of green peas
- 1 cup of blanched sweet corn kernels
- 1 cup of chopped carrots (blanched)
- 1 cup of spinach puree
- 2 cups of mashed and cooked potatoes
- 1 tbsp of oil
- 1 cup of pineapple puree
- 5 tbsp of sugar
- 3 tbsp of lemon juice
- 1 tbsp of cumin seed
- 1 cup of apple puree
- 2 handfuls of chopped onions
- 1 tbsp of salt
- 1 tbsp of cinnamon powder
- 1 tbsp of nutmeg powder

AAAAAAAAAAAAAAAAAAAAAAAA

Methods:

A. In a pot, sauté the cumin seeds and chopped onions for about 2 minutes until the onions become translucent and the cumin releases its aroma.

B. Add all the remaining List of Ingredients (green peas, blanched sweet corn kernels, blanched chopped carrots, spinach puree, mashed and cooked potatoes, oil, pineapple puree, sugar, lemon juice, apple puree, salt, cinnamon powder, and nutmeg powder) to the pot.

C. Cook the soup mixture until all the ingredients are well cooked and the flavors have melded together.

D. Serve the Indian Winter Soup hot and enjoy this flavorful and comforting soup.

Cooking notes:

A. Indian Winter Soup is a hearty and nutritious soup packed with various vegetables and fruits. The soup's sweetness comes from ingredients like pineapple puree, apple puree, and sugar, which balance the savory flavors.

B. To blanch vegetables like carrots and sweet corn kernels, plunge them into boiling water for a short time (1-2 minutes) and then immediately transfer them to ice water to stop the cooking process. This helps retain their vibrant colors and crunchiness in the soup.

C. The spinach puree not only adds a vibrant green color to the soup but also contributes essential nutrients. To make the spinach puree, blanch the spinach leaves and blend them into a smooth paste.

D. Mashed and cooked potatoes act as a thickening agent for the soup, giving it a creamy texture. Cook the potatoes separately until they are soft, then mash them before adding them to the soup.

E. Adjust the amount of sugar and lemon juice according to your taste preference. The soup should have a balanced sweet and tangy flavor.

F. Cinnamon and nutmeg powder add warm and comforting aromas to the soup, enhancing its winter appeal.

G. Serve the Indian Winter Soup as a wholesome and delicious meal on its own or pair it with crusty bread or buttered toast for a satisfying winter dinner.

H. Garnish the soup with chopped fresh herbs like cilantro or parsley for a burst of color and added freshness.

I. This Indian Winter Soup is a versatile recipe, and you can customize it by adding other vegetables or fruits of your choice to suit your taste and seasonal availability.

J. Enjoy this nutritious and flavorful soup to stay warm during the cold winter days!

19. Spiced Veggie Burger

When we say Indians make burgers differently, we mean that in a good way, and this recipe will show you why.

Duration: 10 Minutes

Prep Time: 16 Minutes

Serve: 2

List of Ingredients:

- 1 minced green chili
- 1 minced garlic clove
- 1 pinch of grated ginger
- 1 pinch of garam masala
- 1 pinch of salt
- 2 sliced tomatoes
- 3 lettuce leaves
- 1 handful of sliced onion
- 1 tbsp of oil
- 2 cups of ground chicken
- 1 tsp of ground coriander
- 1 pinch of ground cumin
- 2 handfuls of chopped cilantro
- 4 buns (burger)

AAAAAAAAAAAAAAAAAAAAAAAA

Methods:

A. Preheat the grill to 374 degrees F (190 degrees C). Spray a foil sheet with oil and place it on the grill to prevent the veggie burgers from sticking.

B. In a bowl, combine the ground chicken, minced green chili, minced garlic clove, grated ginger, garam masala, salt, ground coriander, ground cumin, and chopped cilantro. Mix all the ingredients well to evenly distribute the spices and flavors.

C. Shape the mixture into round patties and use a spoon to create a slight indentation in the middle of each patty. This helps the burgers cook evenly and prevents them from puffing up too much during grilling.

D. Arrange the prepared veggie burger patties on the foiled grill and cook them until both sides are well cooked and have reached a safe internal temperature. This may take around 4-5 minutes per side, depending on the thickness of the patties.

E. Assemble the burgers by placing each cooked veggie patty between burger buns. Add sliced tomatoes, lettuce leaves, and sliced onions on top of the patties, or customize the toppings according to your preferences.

F. Serve the Spiced Veggie Burgers while they are still warm and enjoy a flavorful and satisfying plant-based burger option.

Cooking notes:

A. The ground chicken can be substituted with plant-based alternatives like chickpeas, black beans, or lentils to make this a fully vegetarian or vegan-friendly recipe.

B. Adjust the spiciness of the veggie burger by varying the amount of minced green chili used. You can also add other spices or herbs like paprika, turmeric, or parsley for additional flavor.

C. Make sure the grill is preheated to the proper temperature to ensure even cooking of the veggie burgers.

D. Adding chopped cilantro not only enhances the flavor but also provides a nice fresh and herbal touch to the patties.

E. You can toast the burger buns on the grill for a few seconds to add a delicious smoky flavor and extra crunch to the burgers.

F. Serve the spiced veggie burgers with a side of fries, sweet potato wedges, or a fresh salad for a complete and satisfying meal.

G. Experiment with different toppings and condiments like avocado slices, pickles, or your favorite sauce to create your own signature veggie burger.

H. This recipe allows for creativity and adaptability, making it an excellent choice for a delicious and wholesome homemade burger experience. Enjoy your Spiced Veggie Burgers!

20. Kerala Sunset Cocktail

Watch the sunset in Kerala with your special one and enjoy a glass of this cocktail.

Duration: 15 Minutes

Prep Time: Nil

Serve: 2

List of Ingredients:

- 1 pinch of jaggery
- 3 tbsp of lemon juice
- 2 oz of Bombay Sapphire gin
- 4 oz of coconut rum
- 1 tbsp of blue Curaçao
- 1 tbsp of liqueur
- 1 tbsp of beet juice
- 1 tbsp of coconut oil
- 1 tsp of ground fennel seed
- 1 pinch of salt
- 1 cup of ice cubes
- 3 tbsp of ginger beer

For garnishes

- 2 lemon wedges
- 1 handful of rose petals

AAAAAAAAAAAAAAAAAAAAAAA

Methods:

A. In a bowl, combine jaggery, lemon juice, Bombay Sapphire gin, and coconut rum. Mix the ingredients well to ensure they are fully combined.

B. Take the glasses you plan to use for serving the cocktail and coat the rims with the mixture from step 1. This step adds a touch of sweetness and flavor to the rim of the glasses.

C. Place the coated glasses in the refrigerator to chill while you prepare the rest of the drink.

D. In a shaker, combine coconut rum, lemon juice, ice cubes, and Bombay Sapphire gin. Shake the mixture thoroughly to chill and combine the ingredients.

E. Once the mixture is well shaken, strain it into the chilled glasses that have been coated with the jaggery and lemon juice mixture.

F. After pouring the base cocktail into the glasses, carefully add blue Curaçao, liqueur, and beet juice to each glass. These additions give the cocktail its unique colors and enhance the flavor profile.

G. Garnish the cocktails with lemon wedges and rose petals to add a visually appealing and aromatic touch.

H. The Kerala Sunset Cocktail is now ready to be served and enjoyed!

Cooking notes:

A. Jaggery is a traditional Indian sweetener made from sugarcane juice or palm sap. It has a unique flavor profile that adds depth and sweetness to the cocktail. If you can't find jaggery, you can substitute it with brown sugar or another sweetener of your choice.

B. Bombay Sapphire gin is a popular choice for this cocktail due to its aromatic botanicals and smooth taste. However, you can use any other type of gin you prefer.

C. Coconut rum adds a tropical and coconutty twist to the cocktail, enhancing the overall flavor profile.

D. Blue Curaçao is a bright blue liqueur with an orange flavor. It not only adds a stunning blue color to the cocktail but also enhances its citrusy notes.

E. The use of ginger beer adds a spicy kick and effervescence to the cocktail. You can adjust the amount of ginger beer based on your personal preference for spiciness.

F. Beet juice is responsible for the rich sunset-like color of the cocktail. It is also a natural sweetener and complements the other flavors in the drink.

G. The garnishes of lemon wedges and rose petals not only add visual appeal but also provide a delightful aroma that complements the cocktail.

H. Feel free to adjust the proportions of the ingredients to suit your taste preferences. The cocktail can be easily customized based on your liking for sweetness, spiciness, and strength.

I. Enjoy the Kerala Sunset Cocktail responsibly and savor its unique blend of flavors and colors!

21. Jal Jeera Mojito

Need something spicy yet cool for summer? Here it is!

Duration: 05 Minutes

Prep Time: Nil

Serve: 2

List of Ingredients:

- 6 ounces of club soda
- 2 lemon wedges
- 1 tbsp of tamarind chutney
- 1 handful of mint leaves
- 2 handfuls of ice cubes
- 2 tbsp of jaljeera masala mix
- 3 ounces of vodka
- 1 tbsp of lemon juice

AAAAAAAAAAAAAAAAAAAAAAAA

Methods:

A. In a jar, combine the masala mix. The masala mix typically includes cumin powder, black salt, black pepper, dry mango powder (amchur), and other spices that give the Jal Jeera its distinct flavor.

B. Pour soda or sparkling water into the jar. This will add a refreshing fizziness to the drink.

C. Add a spoonful of mint-coriander chutney to the mixture. The chutney enhances the herbal and tangy notes of the drink.

D. Squeeze fresh lemon juice into the jar. The lemon juice provides a zesty and citrusy kick to the Jal Jeera Mojito.

E. Toss in some ice cubes to chill the drink and make it more refreshing.

F. If you desire an alcoholic version, add a shot of vodka to the mixture. This adds a boozy twist to the traditional Jal Jeera.

G. Stir the mixture well to ensure all the flavors are combined.

H. Pour the prepared Jal Jeera Mojito into serving glasses.

I. Garnish the drink with fresh mint leaves and lemon wedges for an appealing presentation.

Cooking notes:

A. The masala mix is the key ingredient that gives Jal Jeera its unique taste. You can find ready-made Jal Jeera masala in stores or prepare it at home by grinding together the required spices.

B. Mint-coriander chutney is a common addition to Jal Jeera and adds a burst of fresh herbal flavors. You can use store-bought chutney or make it at home by blending mint leaves, coriander leaves, green chilies, lemon juice, and a pinch of salt.

C. Adjust the lemon juice, soda, and chutney quantities according to your taste preferences. Some people prefer a stronger lemony taste, while others enjoy a more mild and fizzy drink.

D. For a non-alcoholic version, omit the vodka and stick to soda or sparkling water. The drink will still be delicious and refreshing.

E. Make sure the ingredients are well mixed before serving to ensure an even distribution of flavors.

F. Jal Jeera Mojito is a perfect summer beverage, known for its cooling properties and ability to aid digestion.

G. Feel free to get creative with the garnishes. You can add a slice of cucumber, a sprinkle of chaat masala, or a pinch of roasted cumin powder on top for extra flair.

H. Serve the Jal Jeera Mojito chilled and enjoy its refreshing and flavorful taste!

I. Always drink responsibly, and if serving alcoholic versions, make sure to check the legal drinking age and preferences of your guests.

22. Potato Chicken Curry

Adding potatoes to your chicken curry takes it to a whole new level of chicken curries!

Duration: 10 Minutes

Prep Time: 30 Minutes

Serve: 2

List of Ingredients:

- 1 pinch of salt
- 1 pinch of powdery coriander
- 1 bay leaf
- 1 pinch of red pepper (ground)
- 1 minced ginger
- 1 minced garlic
- 5 ounces of chicken broth
- 1 cup of cubed sweet potatoes (undrained)
- 1 handful of rinsed chickpeas (drained)
- 4 tbsp of green peas
- 1 pinch of ground turmeric
- 1 tsp of curry powder
- 1 pinch of pepper
- 1 pound of boneless chicken breast (skinless and chunked)
- 1 tsp of oil
- 2 handfuls of sliced onions
- 5 ounces of diced tomatoes
- 1 tsp of lemon juice

AAAAAAAAAAAAAAAAAAAAAAAA

Methods:

A. In a bowl, combine coriander, curry powder, salt, black pepper, turmeric, and bay leaf to create the curry spice mixture.

B. In a pan with oil, sauté the chicken pieces until they are lightly browned. This step helps to seal in the juices and adds flavor to the curry.

C. Add the sliced onion to the pan with the chicken and cook for about 6 minutes until the onions become soft and translucent.

D. Stir in the minced garlic and ginger to enhance the curry's aromatic flavors.

E. Toss the curry spice mixture into the pan along with diced tomatoes and chicken broth. Let the mixture simmer and cook for approximately 25 minutes to allow the flavors to meld and the chicken to become tender. Remember to remove the bay leaf after cooking, as it's for flavoring only and not meant to be eaten.

F. Add chickpeas and potatoes to the pan, and continue cooking for an additional 20 minutes until the potatoes are tender and the curry has thickened.

G. As a final touch, add peas to the curry and cook for another 3 minutes. This adds a burst of color and freshness to the dish.

H. Turn off the stove and stir in the lemon juice, which adds a tangy and bright flavor to the curry.

I. Serve the delicious potato chicken curry with your choice of accompaniments, such as rice or bread.

Cooking notes:

A. You can adjust the amount of spices and seasoning according to your taste preferences. Feel free to add more or less of any ingredient to suit your desired level of spiciness and flavor.

B. For a creamier texture, you can add coconut milk or cream to the curry. This will give it a rich and velvety consistency.

C. If you prefer a thicker curry, you can mash some of the cooked potatoes with a fork to help thicken the sauce.

D. Garnish the potato chicken curry with chopped fresh cilantro or parsley to add a pop of color and freshness to the dish.

E. The curry can be refrigerated and reheated the next day, which often enhances the flavors even more.

F. Experiment with different vegetables or proteins in the curry to create variations of the dish. You can try using other meats like lamb or beef, or add vegetables like spinach, bell peppers, or cauliflower for more variety.

G. Adjust the level of spiciness by adding more or less chili powder or using a milder variety of curry powder.

H. Enjoy the warm and comforting flavors of this potato chicken curry with your family and friends!

23. Chickpea Curry Dip

This dip is suitable for all your dip needs.

Duration: 10 Minutes

Prep Time: 10 Minutes

Serve: 2

List of Ingredients:

- 1 tsp of chopped garlic
- 2 handfuls of diced shallot
- 1 tsp of curry powder
- 2 tbsp of lemon juice
- 1 handful of lemon zest
- 7 ounces of coconut milk
- 4 tbsp of coconut oil
- 1 tsp of tomato paste
- 7 ounces of rinsed chickpeas (drained)
- 1 tbsp of salt
- 1 tbsp of pepper

AAAAAAAAAAAAAAAAAAAAAAAA

Methods:

A. Heat oil in a pan and sauté the garlic and shallot until fragrant.

B. Stir in the cumin and curry paste, and cook for about 3 minutes to enhance the flavors.

C. Add the chickpeas and coconut milk to the pan. Let it simmer for approximately 4 minutes to allow the ingredients to blend together.

D. Season the mixture with salt, pepper, freshly squeezed juice (such as lemon or lime), and some citrus zest for added brightness.

E. Serve the chickpea curry dip as a delightful appetizer or snack.

F. Enjoy the dip with your favorite accompaniments like pita bread, tortilla chips, vegetable sticks, or crackers.

Cooking Notes:

A. For the garlic and shallots, finely chop or mince them to release their flavors better in the dish.

B. When adding the cumin and curry paste, stir them well into the oil and aromatics to evenly distribute the spices.

C. To enhance the curry flavor, you can use various curry pastes, such as red, green, or yellow, depending on your preference for spiciness and taste.

D. While simmering the chickpeas in coconut milk, keep an eye on the consistency. If the mixture becomes too thick, you can add a splash of water or vegetable broth to adjust it.

E. Adjust the salt and pepper according to your taste preferences. You can also add other spices or herbs like turmeric, coriander, or cilantro to enhance the flavors further.

F. The citrus juice and zest bring a refreshing element to the dip. Consider using lime, lemon, or even orange to add a tangy twist.

G. Feel free to garnish the dip with some fresh herbs like cilantro or parsley before serving for an appealing presentation.

H. This chickpea curry dip can be prepared ahead of time and stored in the refrigerator. Reheat it gently on the stovetop or in the microwave before serving.

I. If you prefer a creamier texture, you can blend the dip slightly, leaving some chickpeas whole for added texture.

J. Experiment with the level of spiciness by adjusting the amount of curry paste or adding some chili flakes if desired.

24. Curried Carrot Soup

Another vegan recipe for you and your loved one!

Duration: 10 Minutes

Prep Time: 30 Minutes

Serve: 2

List of Ingredients:

- 3 handfuls of chopped celery
- 1 tbsp of canola oil
- 2 minced cloves garlic
- 1 lb. of sliced carrots
- 6 tbsp of rice milk
- 1 cup of chopped onion
- 7 ounces of coconut milk
- 1 pinch of curry powder
- 1 pinch of grated ginger
- 1 tsp of syrup
- 1 tbsp of salt
- 1 tbsp of pepper
- 4 tbsp of carrot juice

To garnish

- 2 handfuls of chopped pistachios
- 2 handfuls of sliced green onions

AAAAAAAAAAAAAAAAAAAAAAAA

Methods:

A. In a pan with oil, sauté the celery, onion, and carrots together until they become tender and slightly browned.

B. Season the vegetables with salt and pepper for added flavor.

C. Add the curry powder and garlic to the pan, allowing the spices to infuse the vegetables.

D. Pour in both types of milk (regular milk and coconut milk) along with the carrot juice into the pan.

E. Puree the entire mixture in a blender until it becomes smooth and creamy in texture.

F. Transfer the pureed soup back to the pan.

G. Stir in the freshly grated ginger and a touch of syrup for a hint of sweetness.

H. Serve the curried carrot soup and garnish it with your choice of garnish ingredients.

Cooking Notes:

A. For sautéing the vegetables, cut them into small, uniform pieces to ensure even cooking and easier blending later.

B. The amount of curry powder you use can vary depending on your preference for spiciness and flavor. Start with a small amount and add more as desired.

C. Be careful when pureeing hot liquids in a blender to avoid splattering. Let the mixture cool slightly, and blend in batches if necessary.

D. Adjust the consistency of the soup by adding more milk or carrot juice if it's too thick or adding vegetable broth if you prefer a thinner soup.

E. The grated ginger adds a fresh and zesty taste to the soup. You can adjust the amount of ginger according to your liking.

F. Consider using maple syrup or honey for the sweetener. Alternatively, you can use agave nectar or brown sugar for a different flavor profile.

G. Popular garnish options for curried carrot soup include chopped fresh cilantro, a dollop of yogurt, a sprinkle of toasted coconut, or a drizzle of cream. These garnishes enhance the visual appeal and taste of the dish.

H. This soup can be served both hot and cold, making it suitable for different seasons and preferences.

I. If you want a more luxurious version, you can finish the soup with a swirl of coconut cream on top before serving.

J. The soup can be stored in the refrigerator for a few days, and it also freezes well for longer-term storage. Reheat gently on the stovetop when ready to serve.

25. Butter Cauliflower Bowls

Creamy

Flavorful

Delicious

Duration: 10 Minutes

Prep Time: 20 Minutes

Serve: 2

List of Ingredients:

- 1 tsp of garam masala
- 1 pinch of ground cumin
- 1 diced sweet onion
- 1 minced garlic clove
- 1 tbsp of salt
- 1 tbsp of pepper
- 1 cup of chicken stock
- 1 chopped cauliflower
- 3 tbsp of chopped cilantro leaves
- 1 tsp of grated ginger
- 1 tbsp of butter
- 4 tbsp of tomato paste
- 1 pinch of chili powder
- 6 ounces of tomato sauce
- 4 tbsp of heavy cream

AAAAAAAAAAAAAAAAAAAAAAAAA

Methods:

A. In a pan with melted butter, sauté the onion and garlic until they become translucent and aromatic.

B. Add the vegetable stock, salt, tomato paste, garam masala, cumin, ginger, and tomato sauce to the pan. Cook this mixture for about 6 minutes to allow the flavors to meld.

C. Once the sauce has simmered, add the cauliflower to the pan. Cook the cauliflower until it becomes tender and easily pierced with a fork.

D. Stir in the cilantro and cream, and continue cooking for an additional 3 minutes to thicken the sauce and incorporate the flavors.

E. Serve the butter cauliflower with rice as a delicious and satisfying meal.

Cooking Notes:

A. For added depth of flavor, consider toasting the spices (garam masala and cumin) briefly in the pan before adding the other ingredients. This can enhance the aroma and taste of the dish.

B. When selecting cauliflower, look for fresh and firm heads with tightly packed florets. Rinse the cauliflower thoroughly and cut it into bite-sized pieces for even cooking.

C. For the cream, you can use heavy cream, half-and-half, or coconut cream depending on your preference and dietary restrictions. Adjust the amount of cream according to how rich and creamy you want the dish to be.

D. If the sauce appears too thick, you can add a splash of vegetable stock or water to achieve your desired consistency.

E. For a spicier version, you can add a pinch of red chili flakes or chopped green chilies to the dish.

F. Garnish the butter cauliflower bowls with some additional fresh cilantro leaves or a sprinkle of toasted almond slices for added texture and visual appeal.

G. This dish is a vegetarian-friendly option, but you can also add protein like cooked chickpeas or tofu to make it more filling.

H. Butter cauliflower bowls can be served as a standalone main course or as a side dish to complement other Indian-inspired dishes.

I. Leftovers can be stored in the refrigerator for a few days and reheated for later meals. The flavors may develop further over time, making it even more delicious when reheated.

J. Enjoy experimenting with the spices and seasoning to suit your taste preferences. You can also add other vegetables like peas, bell peppers, or carrots to make the dish more colorful and nutritious.

26. Curried Cauliflower Soup

Creamy and delicious!!

Duration: 10 Minutes

Prep Time: 15 Minutes

Serve: 2

List of Ingredients:

- 1 minced garlic clove
- 1 diced onion
- 1 tsp of ground turmeric
- 1 pinch of grated ginger
- 6 tbsp of chicken broth
- 1 tsp of ground cumin
- 6 ounces of coconut milk
- 6 ounces of diced tomatoes
- 1 tbsp of pepper
- 1 tbsp of salt
- 1 tsp of oil
- 1 tbsp of curry powder
- 1 pound of crumbled cauliflower

AAAAAAAAAAAAAAAAAAAAAAAA

Methods:

A. In a pan with oil, sauté the onion until it becomes soft and translucent.
B. Add cumin, ginger, garlic, curry, and turmeric to the pan. Cook for about 1 minute to release their flavors.
C. Stir in the tomatoes, coconut milk, cauliflower, and broth. Let the mixture cook and simmer for 15 minutes until the cauliflower becomes tender.
D. Transfer the cooked mixture into a blender and blend until smooth and creamy.
E. Serve the curried cauliflower soup hot and enjoy its flavorful and comforting taste.

Cooking Notes:

A. For the onion, chop it finely to ensure it cooks evenly and blends smoothly later on.

B. When adding the spices (cumin, ginger, garlic, curry, and turmeric), you can toast them briefly in the pan before adding other ingredients to enhance their aroma and taste.

C. Use canned or fresh tomatoes for this soup, depending on what's readily available. If using canned tomatoes, you can choose diced tomatoes or crushed tomatoes for added convenience.

D. The type of curry powder used can vary, so adjust the amount according to your desired level of spiciness and flavor. Feel free to experiment with different curry blends or make your own using various spices.

E. For the coconut milk, you can use either full-fat or light coconut milk based on your preference. The full-fat version will yield a creamier and richer soup.

F. When blending the soup, be cautious with hot liquids. Allow the mixture to cool slightly before blending to avoid any accidents, and blend in batches if needed.

G. After blending, taste the soup and adjust the seasoning as necessary. You can add more salt, pepper, or any other spices to suit your taste.

H. To garnish the soup, consider adding a swirl of coconut milk, a sprinkle of fresh cilantro, or a dash of paprika for a pop of color and added flavor.

I. The soup can be served as a delightful appetizer or paired with crusty bread for a satisfying meal.

J. Leftover soup can be stored in the refrigerator for a few days and reheated on the stovetop when ready to serve. The flavors may intensify and develop further over time.

K. This curried cauliflower soup can be made ahead and frozen for future consumption. Simply thaw and reheat it when needed for a quick and tasty meal.

27. No Yeast Naan

This homemade Naan is better than the store-bought!

Duration: 20 Minutes

Prep Time: 15 Minutes

Serve: 2

List of Ingredients:

- 150g of wheat flour
- 20g of unsweetened yogurt
- 100 ml of lukewarm water (divided)
- 7g of butter
- 2 chopped garlic cloves
- 1 tbsp of Nigella seeds
- 1 pinch of salt
- 1 pinch of baking soda
- 3g of baking powder
- 150g of all-purpose flour

AAAAAAAAAAAAAAAAAAAAAAA

Methods:

A. Preheat a griddle to 423 degrees F (around 220 degrees C).

B. In a bowl, mix together yogurt, 30ml warm water, and baking powder. Set this mixture aside.

C. In another bowl, combine the yogurt mixture, both flours, salt, baking soda, and the remaining warm water. Mix everything well until a smooth dough forms.

D. Cut the dough into pieces and roll each piece out to form flat shapes.

E. Sprinkle garlic and Nigella seeds on the flat dough.

F. Roll the dough again to ensure the garlic and seeds stick well to the dough.

G. Place the prepared dough on the preheated griddle and cook both sides until they are done and have nice golden-brown spots.

H. Once cooked, smear butter on the naan for added flavor and richness.

I. Serve the no yeast naan while still warm for a delicious and delightful accompaniment to your favorite curries or Indian dishes.

Cooking Notes:

A. The griddle should be preheated well before cooking the naan. If you don't have a griddle, you can use a non-stick skillet or a cast-iron pan as an alternative.

B. Make sure the yogurt is at room temperature or slightly warm, as using cold yogurt can affect the dough's texture.

C. You can use plain yogurt or Greek yogurt for this recipe. Greek yogurt may result in a slightly denser naan.

D. Experiment with the flour ratios to achieve the desired texture. You can adjust the amounts of all-purpose flour and whole wheat flour to make the naan softer or chewier.

E. Rolling the dough thin will result in a crispier naan, while a slightly thicker dough will yield a softer naan.

F. Nigella seeds (also known as kalonji or black seeds) add a distinct flavor to the naan. If you don't have them, you can omit or substitute them with sesame seeds or nigella seeds.

G. If the dough sticks to the rolling pin while rolling, lightly dust the rolling pin and the work surface with flour.

H. Keep an eye on the naan while cooking on the griddle to prevent burning. You can lightly press down the naan with a spatula while cooking to help it cook evenly.

I. For added flavor, you can brush the cooked naan with melted garlic butter or sprinkle some fresh chopped cilantro before serving.

J. No yeast naan is a great alternative when you don't have yeast or time for traditional yeast-based naan. It is quick and easy to make and pairs well with various Indian and Middle Eastern dishes.

28. Panagram

Enjoy the flavors of lime and ginger in this tasty Indian drink!

Duration: 04 Minutes

Prep Time: Nil

Serve: 2

List of Ingredients:

- 1 tsp of ground cinnamon
- 1 tsp of lime juice
- 1 handful of ice cubes
- 1 tsp of ginger powder
- 2 tbsp of grated jaggery

AAAAAAAAAAAAAAAAAAAAAAAA

Methods:

A. In a jar, combine the grated jaggery (or brown sugar), ginger powder, ground cinnamon, and boiling water.

B. Stir the mixture well until the jaggery (or sugar) dissolves and the flavors are combined.

C. Place a handful of ice cubes into serving glasses.

D. Strain the prepared mixture into the glasses with ice cubes.

E. Add the lime juice to the glasses.

F. Stir the Panagram drink in each glass to ensure all the flavors are well mixed.

G. Enjoy the refreshing and flavorful Panagram drink immediately.

Cooking Notes:

A. Jaggery is a traditional sweetener commonly used in Indian cuisine. If you can't find jaggery, you can use brown sugar as a substitute.

B. The amount of jaggery (or brown sugar) can be adjusted according to your desired level of sweetness. Taste the mixture as you stir to find the right balance for your palate.

C. Make sure the water is boiling when adding it to the jar to help dissolve the jaggery or sugar more effectively.

D. You can use fresh lime juice for a zesty and tangy flavor, or bottled lime juice if fresh limes are not available.

E. If you prefer a stronger ginger flavor, you can use freshly grated ginger instead of ginger powder. Adjust the quantity based on your taste preferences.

F. For added aroma and visual appeal, you can garnish the drink with a lime wedge or a sprinkle of ground cinnamon before serving.

G. This Panagram drink is best served immediately while the flavors are fresh and vibrant.

H. You can experiment with the drink by adding other spices like cardamom or cloves, or even a splash of coconut milk for a creamy twist.

I. To turn this Panagram into a warm beverage, you can heat the mixture on the stove instead of using boiling water. Once the jaggery (or sugar) is fully dissolved, strain it into the serving glasses with the ice cubes and lime juice, and enjoy a cozy spiced drink.

J. Play around with the proportions to find the perfect balance of sweetness and spice that suits your taste buds. Enjoy this delightful and refreshing Panagram drink as a delicious beverage for any occasion!

29. Carrot Chickpea Curry

We love this meal, and we bet that you and your special one will love it too!

Duration: 15 Minutes

Prep Time: 35 Minutes

Serve: 2

List of Ingredients:

- 40g of grated ginger
- 1 tbsp of chili powder
- 300g of cooked chickpeas
- 200g of coconut milk
- 300g of tomatoes
- 1 tbsp of turmeric (ground)
- 1 tbsp of salt
- 1 tsp of cinnamon (ground)
- 1 pinch of black pepper
- 3 minced garlic clove
- 350g of chopped carrots
- 100g of chopped onion
- 1 tbsp of olive oil
- 1 tbsp of ground coriander
- 1 tbsp of cumin (ground)
- 1 tsp of fenugreek leaves (dried)

AAAAAAAAAAAAAAAAAAAAAAAA

Methods:

A. Sauté the carrots in a pan with oil until they start to soften.

B. In a separate bowl, mix together the spices (curry powder, cumin, coriander, turmeric, and red chili powder). Set the spice mixture aside.

C. Add the chopped onion, ginger, and garlic to the sautéed carrots in the pan. Cook for about 3 minutes until the onions become translucent and the mixture is fragrant.

D. Stir in the combined spice mixture, coating the carrot and onion mixture with the aromatic spices.

E. Add the chickpeas, salt, coconut milk, and diced tomatoes to the pan. Toss in the fenugreek leaves for added flavor.

F. Cover the pan with a lid and let the curry simmer for about 20 minutes, allowing all the flavors to meld together.

G. Serve the delicious carrot chickpea curry and enjoy it as a satisfying and nutritious meal.

Cooking Notes:

A. For the carrots, peel them and chop them into bite-sized pieces for even cooking.

B. The choice of oil for sautéing can be vegetable oil, coconut oil, or any other cooking oil you prefer.

C. When mixing the spices in the bowl, consider using a teaspoon of each spice or adjust the quantities based on your preferred level of spiciness and flavor.

D. If you like your curry milder, you can reduce the amount of red chili powder or omit it altogether.

E. For the chickpeas, you can use canned chickpeas (garbanzo beans) for convenience or cook dried chickpeas ahead of time. If using canned chickpeas, make sure to drain and rinse them thoroughly before adding them to the curry.

F. Coconut milk adds richness and creaminess to the curry. You can use either full-fat or light coconut milk based on your preference.

G. If you don't have fenugreek leaves, you can omit them, or replace them with spinach or kale for added greens.

H. Taste the curry as it cooks and adjust the seasoning as needed. You can add more salt or spices according to your taste preferences.

I. To make the curry even more nutritious, you can add other vegetables like spinach, peas, or bell peppers.

J. This carrot chickpea curry pairs well with steamed rice, quinoa, or flatbreads like naan or roti.

K. Leftovers can be refrigerated and reheated for later meals. The flavors may develop further over time, making it even more delicious when reheated.

L. Enjoy experimenting with the spices and seasoning to suit your taste preferences. Carrot chickpea curry is a flavorful and hearty vegetarian dish that is easy to prepare and perfect for both lunch and dinner.

30. Indian Summer Salad

Salad in summer… let's just say Summery Salad.

Duration: 10 Minutes

Prep Time: Nil

Serve: 2

List of Ingredients:

- 1 handful of sliced radishes
- 2 grated carrots
- 1 handful of chopped red onion
- 3 tbsp of dressing
- 1 handful of shredded mint leaves
- 1 sliced courgette

AAAAAAAAAAAAAAAAAAAAAAAA

Methods:

A. In a bowl, combine the sliced radishes, grated carrots, chopped red onion, shredded mint leaves, and sliced courgette (zucchini).

B. Mix all the ingredients well to ensure they are evenly distributed and the flavors are combined.

C. Serve the Indian Summer Salad with a drizzle of your favorite dressing to add extra taste and moisture.

D. Enjoy this refreshing and vibrant salad as a delicious and healthy addition to any meal.

Cooking Notes:

A. Feel free to customize this Indian Summer Salad with additional vegetables or ingredients. You can add diced cucumbers, bell peppers, or cherry tomatoes for extra crunch and color.

B. For the dressing, you can use a variety of options, such as a classic vinaigrette, yogurt-based dressing, or a lemon-honey dressing for a tangy twist. Choose a dressing that complements the flavors of the vegetables and herbs used in the salad.

C. When slicing the radishes, carrots, and courgette (zucchini), try to maintain uniform thickness for a consistent texture in each bite.

D. Grating the carrots adds a delicate texture to the salad and helps distribute their sweetness throughout.

E. Red onions add a mild spiciness to the salad, but you can also use shallots or green onions for a different flavor profile.

F. Shredded mint leaves contribute a refreshing and aromatic element to the salad. Make sure to tear the mint leaves gently to release their natural oils.

G. This Indian Summer Salad can be served as a side dish with grilled meats, fish, or as part of a vegetarian spread. It is also perfect for picnics, potlucks, or as a light lunch option.

H. Consider sprinkling some toasted nuts or seeds like almonds, sunflower seeds, or pumpkin seeds on top of the salad for added texture and nutrition.

I. The salad can be made ahead of time, but it is best to add the dressing just before serving to keep the vegetables crisp and prevent the salad from becoming soggy.

J. For a creamy variation, you can toss the salad with some Greek yogurt or a yogurt-based dressing.

K. This Indian Summer Salad is rich in vitamins and fiber, making it a nutritious and delightful addition to your summer menu. Enjoy the mix of fresh and colorful ingredients for a burst of flavors and textures in every bite.

See You Again

Thank you for purchasing and reading my book. Your support means a lot, and I'm grateful you chose my book among many options. I write to help people like you, who appreciate every word.

Please share your thoughts on the book, as reader feedback helps me grow and improve. Your insights may even inspire others. Thanks again!

Printed in Great Britain
by Amazon

27688169R00064